Conquering Health Anxiety

How to Break Free from the Hypochondria Trap

By Darren Sims

Important Legal Disclaimer

The guidance provided in this book reflects the author's opinions and should by no means be used to replace medical advice.

Before making any dietary or lifestyle changes, consult your physician or GP. The publisher and author are not responsible for any loss, damages or negative consequences that may occur as a result of following the information in this book.

References are provided for informational purposes only and should not be considered to be endorsements. Please note the websites provided are accurate at the time of writing and may change.

Table of Contents

Introduction: Escaping the Hypochondria Trap

Leaf through today's newspaper or browse your favourite news website and I'm willing to place a bet that you'll pick up a fair selection of health-related articles. Perhaps it's a new diet to fend off diabetes, tips to keep your skin looking bright and beautiful, a food ingredient that has been proven to cause cancer, or perhaps a weird and wonderful bird influenza that's slowly flapping its way over here from some remote village in South-East Asia.

You cannot deny it; we are all pretty preoccupied with our health and wellbeing. We want to find ways to live longer and feel better, whether that's through diet or lifestyle changes. The good news is that this obsession is somewhat paying off; we are certainly living longer than ever – just take a look at the mortality rates published by the Office of National Statistics.

As bright and cheery as this all sounds, one difficulty is that this increased awareness of medical symptoms and conditions has also led to a heightened sense of health anxiety for many of us. How many times have you experienced a symptom and 'googled' it before going to visit your GP? If you're like me, you may well have lost count! The trouble with this approach is that a mere headache can lead to a self-diagnosis of anything ranging from a migraine to a life-threatening brain tumour.

This book is about health anxiety, from the viewpoint of someone who has suffered – and near enough recovered – from it. Please take note that I am not a medical professional and the information I share is meant to serve as advice, rather than a medical assessment. However, I do hope that my own interpretation of health anxiety and sharing my own ways out of it will assist those of you currently battling this debilitating condition.

In this book I would like to show you the techniques that helped me knock my health anxiety into the ground. It is my hope that you too can use some of these ideas to pull yourself out of the hypochondria trap.

At the forefront of pushing health anxiety out of your life is changing your thinking patterns. This may sound challenging at first but trust me, it's easier than it looks – though it certainly takes an amount of dedication and self-reflection.

As serious as health anxiety can be, my purpose is to reach out to you in a way that's light-hearted. When you're in the throes of anxiety, it may seem like the world is crashing down all around you. But when you manage to navigate past those rocky seas, it's a lot easier to look back and laugh about some of the things that seemed to be plaguing your thoughts and ruining your life before.

Perhaps you have bought this as you, or someone close to you, suffers from health anxiety. Maybe you're a student who wishes to learn more about this condition from someone who has suffered from it firsthand. In any case, I hope that this e-Book provides value to you. If you have any questions or would like to give feedback, please do not hesitate to contact me at info@healthanxietyhelp.com.

Part 1: How All This Crap Began

"After obsessively Googling symptoms for four hours, I discovered 'obsessively Googling symptoms' is a symptom of hypochondria."
Stephen Colbert

Over the past ten years I've been diagnosed with multiple sclerosis, several brain tumours, meningitis, diabetes, pneumonia, stomach cancer, a burst appendix, testicular cancer, epilepsy, way too many heart attacks to count, a brain aneurysm, avian flu and vCJD (the human version of Mad Cow Disease.)

If you bumped into me in the street, however, you might think that I look pretty well.

I guess that's because I left a small piece of information out; when I say I was 'diagnosed' I don't mean by a qualified doctor. Certainly not. In fact it's quite incredible - none of the GPs I encountered over the years seemed at all concerned by the symptoms I mentioned to them; not the twitching hands, the stomach pains or even the heart palpitations which surely meant that I was on the verge of having a heart attack. So in the end what other choice did I have to diagnose myself?

Does any of this sound familiar? To tell the honest truth, I have had none of the life-threatening conditions I listed above. Instead, what I *have* suffered from is health anxiety. As the name suggests, it involves an awful lot of worrying about your health – often to the point where it affects other parts of your life; relationships, your job performance, lifestyle habits and sometimes even your physical health.

However, I am pleased to say that now, after seven or eight years, health anxiety is no longer the bane of my existence that it used to be. I would be lying if I told you that I no longer worry about my health at all; if I have a sudden sharp chest pain, I will certainly briefly entertain the idea of a heart attack. However, it is no longer something that controls me and stops me doing things that I want to do. In fact, my life has completely changed since I conquered my health anxiety. I am now married, have a challenging yet rewarding job and live a healthy, balanced lifestyle (with a slight partiality towards takeaway pizza from time to time.) But it certainly took some time to get here.

In this chapter I would like to tell my story, right from the very start. I hope that some of it resonates with some of you and most importantly helps you to see that you're not alone in this.

*

It all began in October. And it was an October like no other. I had just celebrated my 21st birthday with my closest relatives and friends,

I was halfway through my University course and was pretty darn excited about the future.

Unfortunately this excitement turned out to be short-lived, as my then-girlfriend's mother suddenly and unexpectedly passed away due to complications from a lung infection. She was young, too – only 48. It was a hard time for both my ex-girlfriend and I.

This traumatic event also got me thinking. If she died at such a young age, who could say that the same thing wouldn't happen to me, at age 21? Sure, I figured I was reasonably healthy and it was unlikely that I would drop dead in the street. But what if it *did* happen?

I began to focus obsessively on these thoughts on a daily basis and, although I could go about most of my business, I had this deep, underlying belief that something bad could happen to me at any moment.

And it did, just not quite in the way that I expected.

I had just spent an hour or so in the University computer lab slaving away at an assignment. It was a mild Summer evening so I decided to walk home, as my student accommodation was only a short distance away.

Ambling back down the road, I suddenly felt a short, sharp twinge in my stomach. My mind raced: *What could it be? Was it gas? Was it appendicitis? Was it the spicy Indian curry I had eaten the night before? My liver? No wait, it's not my stomach – it's my heart!*

This sense of panic lasted for a minute or so. Whatever it was, I was utterly convinced that I was about to die. In fact, as I turned into the road leading to my flat, I started picturing myself keeling over right there and then. My breathing was laboured; my lungs didn't seem to be taking in air like they should. My heartbeat was racing and my skin felt prickly and hot.

I darted over to a nearby bench and sat with my head in my hands. I tried to breathe slowly but the more I focused on my breathing, the worse it all seemed to get.

So I ran, as fast as my legs would take me. I bolted up to the University reception and could barely get out what I was trying to say as I was so out of breath.

"Something's wrong," I panted. "Something's wrong with me!"

The security guard's response was alarmingly casual.

"Come round here and take a seat," he muttered, opening the office door round the side.

I walked in and he invited me to take a seat in the chair, at which point he got me a glass of water.

Before I knew it, I noticed that my breathing was slowly but surely returning to normal. The stomach pains that had set me off just moments before had disappeared completely.

"You're the second person who's run in here this week saying the same thing," he joked, as he handed me a piece of his chocolate bar.

After 10 minutes or so, I walked back to my dorm room with my tail between my legs, feeling shocked and totally confused as to what had just happened to me.

It wasn't for some time that I realised that I had experienced my first panic attack. Unfortunately, it was the first of many to come, as a result of my health anxiety.

Things soon became worse. After this first panic attack, I would focus on the smallest symptoms and attribute them to something incurable and life-threatening.

Headache? That's a brain tumour. Stomach pain? Stomach cancer. Racing heartbeat? Easy – that's got to be a heart attack.

I recall at one point I was absolutely focused on a small muscle twitch in my foot. I immediately searched for the symptom on the internet and was presented with a list of colourful diagnoses to choose from, ranging from brain disorders to vitamin deficiencies. Of course my health anxiety censored out all of the harmless possibilities and focused on the life-threatening ones.

I reached one of my lowest points in Christmas that year. I was due to be spending that time with my ex-girlfriend, who had recently moved about 300 miles away to Lincolnshire, in the North of England. It was her first Christmas without her mother. I badly wanted to be up there with her to console her and be strong for her. The only trouble was, I was a complete and utter wreck. At this point, I could barely go a day without having a nasty panic attack, and I knew that was the last thing that she needed with the genuine trauma that she had been through herself.

After much deliberation, I decided to spend that Christmas with my own parents and family.

On what many consider that most wonderful time of the year, I was profoundly miserable. I opened up my presents on Christmas morning thinking that this would be my last ever Christmas, as there was no doubt in my mind that I would die from an illness the following year.

On Boxing Day, I woke up with terrible stomach pains. I thought it might be appendicitis. I demanded that my parents take me to the local NHS walk-in centre, which was miraculously open. The nurses took one look at me and assured me that it was simply stomach gas. But I was so completely convinced that something was drastically wrong with me, I couldn't believe what I was hearing.

My anxiety issues were affecting every part of my life: in particular my social and family life. My parents were incredibly considerate and patient, but after so many anxiety flare-ups they started getting worn out by my behaviour. At one low point, I asked my mother to take a look at my stools as I was convinced I could see a trace of blood. As you can probably imagine, she saw no sign of blood.

It was around then that I, and those closest to me, thought it was about time that I saw a doctor.

I went to see my GP. I was told that all the symptoms I had been experiencing could be attributed to anxiety and that there were two primary paths I could take: medication and therapy. The ideal situation would be a combination of the two, so that's what I opted for. I was prescribed a box of 'happy pills' and a two-month consultation with a councillor at my University.

In all honesty, I found the counselling sessions to be of little help. In our weekly meetings, my counsellor would make me feel extremely self-conscious, which increased my anxiety further. She seemed to have absolutely no concept of why I couldn't snap out of these convictions I had set for myself. She wanted to know all about my childhood and my relationship with my parents. I told her I had a very happy childhood and I get on very well with both of my parents. It all seemed to fall on deaf ears.

My medication that I was prescribed didn't seem to do much good either – in fact all it seemed to do was make me very sleepy and erratic. Feeling dissatisfied with my lack of progress, I gave up on both the counselling sessions and the medication. It all felt so useless.

My girlfriend and I split up in the Summer. She couldn't take it anymore and I equally had no time for her. I was too wrapped up in my own little 'illnesses' to care for someone else. It was a lonely time; I stopped going out with friends as I was too fearful of having a panic attack in public and I would avoid family get togethers, coming up with a multitude of excuses not to attend. I'd spend my days at home, either on the Internet or lazing around in my bed.

It is difficult to convey in words quite how intense my health anxiety feelings were. It wasn't simply a case of worrying that I had a serious illness; it felt like I had been given an official diagnosis by a GP.

I would hop between doctors, unhappy with how I'd been treated by each one. I would only be satisfied when they suggested getting a medical assessment, such as a blood test. Yet, when the tests came back negative, I would question the ability of the medical staff, or perhaps the efficiency of the test, and I'd be right back at step one again with another GP.

After I graduated from University in 2004, I was lucky enough to find a job soon afterwards – a cushy Accounts position working for the local government. I really enjoyed the work and got along well with my colleagues. But as my anxiety and panic attacks grew more intense, I found it increasingly hard to concentrate and I did not want to participate in work social events.

I was also becoming more and more depressed with my condition. I would often find it hard to sleep at night, I lost interest in almost everything I used to enjoy, such as music and playing five-a-side football, and felt like I was living in a complete haze. Some days I just couldn't face up to going into work and would call in sick.

One day, after about six months in my new job, my manager called me into her office to inform me that unless my performance and attendance improved, I would have to look for another position.

I was heartbroken. Devastated. I felt completely out of control. But this was something of an awakening; it made me realise just how serious my health anxiety had become.

I decided that enough was enough. I simply wasn't enjoying life anymore. I booked in to see my GP again the following day. And I have to say, I consider that one of the days that put me back on track.

As apprehensive as I was, I explained in great detail how I'd been feeling; that anxiety about my health was taking over my life and that I had to do something about it.

Unlike my previous attempts at getting professional help with my anxiety, I felt like I was finally on to something. The doctor seemed concerned; not with any of the symptoms I was experiencing but at the extent to which anxiety was affecting my day-to-day activities.

So, once again, on the doctor's orders I started a new course of anti-depressants and I booked in to a therapist. This time it was related to cognitive-behavioural therapy, something I had not tried before.

I have to admit, I was extremely skeptical about either working, considering my previous experience. But I tried to put that behind me and try again.

To my surprise, my first appointment with the therapist really helped. She was approachable and friendly, and made me feel like I wasn't completely insane (just slightly!) Cognitive behavioural therapy helped to recognise my thinking patterns and work on methods to change them. By the end of my first session, I was laughing about my problem to my therapist.

I recounted a tale to her about a time I went to the bathroom after finishing dinner and looked at my tongue in the mirror. It had turned an unsightly dark shade of red. Of course I started panicking and went straight to the internet. A quick search on Google led me to so many different and awful possibilities... cancer, HIV, bacteria growing on my tongue! I was in the middle of pulling my hair out, speculating on how many days I had to live when my brother piped up from the other room.

"Darren, are you going to finish your red wine or can I have it?"

Red wine. Of course! I picked up my toothbrush from the side of the bathroom sink and gave my tongue a quick brush. No surprises; the dark red patch vanished. I felt like such a numpty at the time and recounting this tale to this day makes me realise how irrational health anxiety can make us!

The key benefit of seeing a therapist was that I had someone to open up to completely. I didn't have to lie or play down my emotions. My therapist also encouraged me to keep a journal, which is something I continue to this day, and continues to help me make sense of my feelings.

My progress made me take a look at all of the aspects of my life; the things I felt were working, as well as those that needed improvement. Several fellow anxiety-sufferers who I met on internet forums had sworn by the benefits of exercise, meditation and a well thought-out meal plan, so I began to read up on these areas and implement them into my daily life.

It was my family who first saw the the improvements. I remember one evening my mother came back from work and questioned me on what was going on. I asked her what she meant. "You seem to be different tonight," she said. "You seem... very chilled out!"

It was not something I noticed immediately but over the coming months my anxiety gradually improved. Don't let me mislead you - it was not an overnight miracle, but the continued counselling and medication seemed to be actually working.

After six months I asked my GP about cutting down on the medication. I had my reservations. My therapy had finished but I was feeling a lot happier in myself and ready to see if I could do this completely by myself.

Soon enough, I was no longer taking medication and controlling anxiety totally by myself. What a feeling that was, knowing that I was in control of my life. When I started having anxious thoughts, I knew exactly what to do to stop them in their tracks – it was almost like playing a game of 'whack-a-mole' with my anxiety!

And that leads us to today. It's been a long time since I stopped taking anti-depressants for anxiety and I'm hopeful that I will never need them again. It hasn't been an easy journey. I have slipped a couple of times, and still have the occasional panic attack. I have learnt that it's something I may well be predisposed to and could have them for the rest of my life – however, I have learnt not to let my anxiety rule my life.

Rather, my anxiety is something of a quirk that rears its ugly head every once in a while but can *always* be beaten back down with a big stick.

I hope that those of you who suffer from health anxiety can relate to parts of my story. You may be at the start of it, like I was at age 21. Or you may be exploring options such as medication and therapy and wanting to look at methods that can compliment these techniques. In the second part of this book, I will outline the steps I personally used to beat health anxiety and start living life to the fullest – and how this will hopefully help you.

Part 2: How To Beat Health Anxiety Down With A Big Stick

"It is the set of the sails, not the direction of the wind that determines which way we will go"

Jim Rohn

First and foremost, I would like to state that the absolute first step in recovery, if you feel that health anxiety is ruining your life, is to contact your GP.

There is really no reason to feel afraid or hesitant about talking about your anxiety issues; these days doctors are highly equipped to discuss mental health issues and will be happy to talk through the options available to you. When going to see your doctor for the first time, you may find it helpful to write a list of the symptoms you have experienced, and how you feel that health anxiety is affecting your life. Be honest, though. Don't understate how you feel. As health anxiety sufferers we can be fantastic actors; we can be all smiles, even though we're cracking up inside.

In this section I will outline several areas that personally helped me tackle health anxiety. We will go through some exercises together as well; if you feel skeptical or wonder if any of this stuff really works, I ask that you bear with me and see it through to the end.

So, if you're ready, please turn the page and let's start this journey together.

Visualising an Anxiety-Free Future

If you're a health anxiety sufferer, I'd like to say with the greatest conviction that you are already a master of visualisation. You may think I'm a complete crackpot but do hear me out.

Let me give you an example; if you're anxious about a bad headache, what do you *visualise* is wrong with you? Something that will clear up in a day or two, or something far more serious? I'd be willing to place a hefty bet on the second option, if you're anything like I used to be.

The truth is that visualisation is very powerful. The trouble is, more often than not we tend to visualise negative situations. For example, have you ever been to a job interview, or perhaps a first date, and even before the event took place you visualised a negative outcome? We're all guilty of it – not just anxiety sufferers. The trouble is with negative visualisation is that we start behaving like the outcome has already happened. If you walk into an interview convinced that you're going to flunk it, it's unlikely that you'll carry the positive body language required from your prospective employer to give a good first impression. You'll maybe slump in, tense up your shoulders, talk without conviction and authority - and before you know it, your visualisation has become a reality.

Well, I've got a question for you. If it's so easy to visualise a bad outcome, and to start acting like this has already happened, do you suppose that we can do the same for something positive? Could visualising an anxiety-free life actually reduce our anxiety? The simple answer is: yes, of course.

For these exercises, read the short brief before following the instructions at the end. You will need a notebook and a pen to hand, as I'd like you to write a few things down after the exercise.

Exercise 1: A Happy Moment

First of all, make sure you are in a quiet place, with no distractions. Put your phone away, switch the TV off, and give this a shot.

What I want you to do is to close your eyes and think back to a time you were positive, relaxed or optimistic. A happy moment. Maybe you were spending time with a loved one, or on holiday. It doesn't matter how long ago it was; yesterday, last week, or 20 years ago. Perhaps it was a time when you were a child.

No matter how long ago it was, try to remember *exactly* how you felt, physically and emotionally. Don't put too much thought into how you feel – just relax in reliving this happy moment. Feel free to smile or laugh out loud as you do it, and at the same time don't worry if your mind wanders a little; slowly and gently bring your thoughts back to this sheer sense of bliss.

Try this for just five minutes. When you have finished turn the page and try the next step.

Finished? Great! So, after that five minutes, how do you feel? Take your notebook (or at the very least a sheet of paper if you can't find a book) and write down the answer to the following question.

If you could sum up your emotions during those five minutes, what three words would you use? (i.e. happy, confident, relaxed.)

Use whatever words you feel are most appropriate. Sometimes words may be hard to come by; if you can't think of any words you might decide to draw or sketch how you felt. That's okay too. Don't spend too long on writing this down – a minute or two should be fine. Once you're done, let's move on to the next exercise.

Exercise 2: A Crappy Moment

Close your eyes and instead of going back to the positive time from before, I want you to recall a moment you were feeling extremely anxious. Go back to a moment when your anxiety was at its absolute peak. I'm guessing it could have been a major panic attack you had in public, or a time when you were alone and bowled over with worry about your health. Think about what it was that worried you at that time.

As with the previous exercise, I want you to think about this for five minutes. Remember – try to immerse yourself in the moment. It's okay if you feel upset, anxious or panicky. It won't be for long.

When the five minutes are up, please turn over the page.

So how did this visualisation feel? A bit different to the previous one I'm guessing! As before, answer the following question, either in words or pictures:

If you could sum up your emotions during those five minutes, what three words would you use? (i.e. worried, panicky, numb.)

So what we've done in these two exercises is to visualise the past. A happy memory and one filled with anxiety. The past is important; but it's just as important to remember that the past need not shape our destiny. Let's move on to the future.

Exercise 3: A Future With Anxiety

I want you to close your eyes once more. This time, I want you to see yourself in five years' time. Imagine that you are staring into a mirror, looking at your reflection. But what I want you to do is this: imagine that you have <u>never</u> recovered from your health anxiety.

Imagine that your anxiety has not only remained but become worse over the five years. Notice how you look – do you look a lot older? Are there bags under your eyes with all the stress and anxiety? How do you feel about yourself as you look at yourself in the mirror?

It's okay to feel sad as you visualise this. It's okay to be upset.

Let yourself visualise this future for five minutes and turn the page.

Sometimes this can be a powerful awakening. I remember when I first tried it at the height of anxiety I burst into tears. As I say, it's okay to be upset by this but remember: this doesn't have to be the future. You have the power to change this. You may well have been fighting anxiety for the last five years – it doesn't mean that you have to be for the next five.

In your notebook, please write a few sentences answering the following question:

If I let anxiety control me in five years' time, how will this affect my life?

You might want to write about how it will affect your relationships, your career plans, your social life. Will you be sleeping well or waking up early and worrying about your health?

Once you've finished writing this, turn the page and let's move on to the final exercise.

Exercise 4: A Future Without Anxiety.

Just as before, close your eyes and imagine yourself in front of a mirror in five years' time.

Only this time, your life is no longer controlled by your anxiety: <u>you</u> are the one in control of your life. You can do all of the things you want to do in life without worrying about panic attacks and silly diseases. You've stopped checking for symptoms on the internet – you have realised that there is *so* much more to life than that.

You are so content with life and proud of yourself at your own recovery, as are the people around you who love you. Feel free to talk out loud about how happy you are. Feel free to laugh. Feel free to sing out loud. Whatever is natural for you.

Remain in this place for five minutes (or longer if you'd like, I'm not going to stop you!) and when you finish, turn the page.

See, visualisation isn't all that hard, is it? I hope that it has given you a sense of inspiration on how you can change. Do you want to spend the next five years with the dull cloud of health anxiety lingering around your head? Or do you want to get your life back?

In the next section, we will discuss thought patterns associated with health anxiety – particularly how to identify them and ultimately how to change them.

Identify and change your thought patterns

So are you still with me? I hope so. Because now we're going to take a closer look into what triggers your health anxiety, and of course what we can do about it.

It is clear that our thoughts, how we react to them and our emotions are all closely linked up, and understanding how they work together is one of the biggest keys to recovering from anxiety.

For most of us, we don't think too much about our thought patterns. As health anxiety sufferers, this can often mean that we're stuck in an ongoing loops, where we're not consciously aware of what is triggering our anxiety, or indeed what behaviour we engage in which serves to reinforce our misconceptions about what is actually happening to us.

In attempting to change your thinking patterns, it's important that you get into the habit of paying close attention to your thoughts. I feel that it is always helpful to write things down, in terms of both making sense of your thoughts as well as seeing the progress that you have achieved in the future. So once again, I recommend writing in your notebook or on a piece of paper (just make sure that it doesn't end up stuffed away at the back of a drawer somewhere!)

Step 1: Identify your thoughts

The first thing we need to do is to find out exactly what we are thinking when we are in our anxious state. To do this, I would like you to think back to a recent situation in which your health anxiety was at its peak. It may be the same occasion as in our visualisation exercise in the previous chapter, or possibly another time when you felt extremely anxious about your health.

With this in your mind, I would like you to answer the following questions:

1. What was going through your mind when you first started to feel anxious? (*i.e. I was worried that my heart was beating fast after walking up the stairs.*)

2. What symptoms did you experience? (*i.e. My heart was racing, I was out of breath and I started sweating.*)

3. What was the absolute worst thing you thought might happen to you? (*i.e. I thought I was going to have a heart attack.*)

Spend no more than five minutes answering these questions, before moving on to the next step.

Step 2: How Do You React?

Here we can go deeper into what specifically makes us worried about our health, in terms of how we perceive the symptoms we experience. In your notebook, I would recommend drawing a table similar to the one in Figure 1.

When filling in the table, start by thinking about recent situations. Try to remember the situations clearly and exactly what symptoms you were worried about.

Fig. 1

Date	Symptom	Anxiety scale	How did you react?	Assumption
22nd August	Deep itch in stomach	7	I checked medical websites I kept prodding and rubbing my stomach	I have liver disease.

You may have a long list of specific situations when you were worried about your health, or you may only be able to think of a couple. In any case, try to fill the table in accurately, before moving on to the next step.

Step 3: Finding an alternative

So now we understand a little bit more about our thought patterns, its time to discover what alternatives we can come up with. Rather than accepting them, it's time to question these exaggerated and nonsensical thoughts! If someone came up to you and told you that an alien had just been spotted walking around the city, I have no doubts that you'd question that person's integrity – and perhaps their sanity!

We really need to be able to do the same with our own internal health anxiety dialogue. When that little voice is nagging at you, constantly telling you that you have a serious disease, you need to scrutinise what he or she is telling you and examine other options.

Here's an example: I wake up with a headache and my 'internal doctor' is trying to persuade me that it's a brain tumour. What alternative options could I present myself that aren't life-threatening?

— It's just a normal headache and will pass.

— I must've slept terribly last night.

— I must've drunk a little bit too much red wine last night.

— Yesterday was a stressful day. No wonder I have a headache today.

— Maybe I've been spending way too long staring at the computer screen recently!

If we present ourselves with a variety of different options, then it becomes a lot harder for our brain to settle on just one. So, what I would like you to do is to complete the following exercise. What we will do is 'juggle' up our anxious thoughts a little, and to connect with different options – different thinking patterns that we can use instead of assuming the single worst case scenario.

What I'd like you to do, to begin with, is to work with one of the situations you identified in the last step. Using this, I would like you to think about some possible alternatives that you may have. Using the two column table provided below in Figure 2, please fill in the information.

It may seem hard to begin with; after all, your internal doctor is extraordinarily convincing and really doesn't want you to change. He'd be out of a job for starters!

If you are struggling, why don't you think of what *someone else* may suggest as an alternative thought. It could be a friend or family member that you think highly of, or even a real GP – what do you realistically think they would suggest as alternatives?

Fig. 2

Symptom	Worrying thought	Possible alternatives
Deep itch in stomach	I have liver disease and I'm going to have to spend months in hospital.	Stomach pain can be caused by anxiety — it will be gone by tomorrow.
		My tummy's just full — I really shouldn't have eaten all that food last night!

The great thing about this is that you can use this any time you feel anxious. It can help provide you with ways to see various options, and shifting your focus away from the debilitating, anxious ones.

Now we are getting somewhere. We have identified our thought patterns and we have learned how to present ourselves with several alternatives. What we can do in the final step is to put it all together, so that in the future you can remind yourself to throw a spanner in the works when you see that your anxious thoughts are rearing their heads.

Step 4: Anxiety-Free Action Statements

So we have taken a look at our existing thought patterns, and come up with (hopefully) several possible alternatives. Now it's time to put your plan into action. One way we can do this is to write out action statements.

At the height of my anxiety, I had a handful of specific health worries that I would constantly obsess over. So, I decided to write five action statements and pin them to my fridge. If you would like to keep them in a more discreet place, that's up to you – but make sure they're written somewhere that you'll see them. Not tucked away at the back of your bedside cabinet!

You can write your own action plan statements using the following structure:

The next time I _____, I will NOT
_____. Instead, I will
_____.

So, for example, one of my personal action plan statements was:

The next time I get a <u>headache</u>, I will NOT <u>assume it's brain cancer</u>. Instead, I will <u>assume it's because I'm tired</u>.

The great thing is, you can make this as general, specific or as utterly nuts as you want. For example, you might say:

The next time I worry about my <u>health</u>, I will NOT <u>check the Internet for symptoms</u>. Instead, I will <u>jump up and down and shout "I'm fine! I'm fine!"</u> Maybe this is one to do when not many people are around!

There is something in writing these statements down that makes your plan more solid, and certainly more achievable.

One way I would remember my statements was printing them out on small flashcards, which I would keep in my wallet. If I was feeling anxious about my health in a public place; say, for example, when I was out for dinner with a friend, I would quickly head to the toilet and take a look at the flashcard just to reassure myself. It may sound crazy, but it worked for me and it may work for you too.

So, we've reached the end of the chapter. Well, that wasn't so bad, was it? While visualisation and changing your thinking patterns are powerful ways of assisting with you health anxiety, there are several other lifestyle habits that you can take on to make a positive impact on your recovery.

Part 3: A Few Lifestyle Changes to Consider

In looking at some of these areas, you may well find that your brain is telling you that you don't need to worry about it. That it's too much effort. That it's a waste of time. In all honesty, that's the same part of your mind that is continually making you anxious about your health – and in doing so, limiting your life. So I think it's time to say goodbye to that little voice once and for all. If you find that after a few months these tips don't work for you that's fine – but I'd suggest that they're at least worth a try. Right?

Your Writing Ritual

You may be wondering what on Earth you're going to do with the other blank pages in your notebook. Well, now all shall be revealed!

As I have commented a number of times in this book, one of the most important things you can do to help yourself understand your own thoughts is to write things down.

The writing ritual is something that was recommended to me by a friend. I have always found it best to do it first thing in the morning, before your brain has had a chance to absorb everything the day brings. But it's really fine to do it at any time. Just make sure you have a spare 20 minutes without being disturbed. That means leaving your smartphone in the other room and turning off the TV!

You may be thinking "15 minutes out of my busy schedule?! No way!" Well, I've got to be honest with you – recovering from health anxiety is a little like practicing a sport, or learning a musical instrument. It's something you need to *work on over time.* If you give someone a trumpet and say to them "take this back home and <u>hope</u> that one day you'll be a maestro!" would you rank their chances? Probably not!

Investing a little time each day is undoubtedly one of the greatest things you can do. So put in your 15 minutes. If you don't have enough time before work, set your alarm just a little earlier. Or if you want to write your journal at lunch time, or in the evening, that's fine too. Just make sure you find that interrupted time. After all, it's time invested in yourself. You deserve it.

In your journal, you can write about anything. That's right – simple as that! Of course, you can write about your health anxiety and other problems, but you needn't restrict it to that. The contents of your journal can be about <u>anything you want</u>.

There are a couple of rules: don't think too much about it and don't stop until you've finished. If you have a large, A4 sized notebook I recommend writing two sides. If you have a smaller book I'd say that three sides is usually enough. It doesn't matter how much you write – simply that your pen doesn't leave the page for the 15 minutes.

It may not be easy at first. You might find yourself writing less than a page. That's okay. Fill the rest of the page up with drawings and sketches.

The key is to let your thoughts guide you. It doesn't matter if it's grammatically incorrect, if there are spelling mistakes or if it's complete and utter gibberish. It's simply a way of getting all the things in your head on to paper.

I have found this such an invaluable way of dealing with things on my mind that I have continued my writing ritual to this day. Over the past five years I think I have skipped maybe three or four, either due to being ill or being in an overseas hotel with no access to a writing pad - it is simply a part of my day now. I'm happy to miss my morning coffee – but never my writing ritual. As a result, I have accumulated years' worth of journals. Sometimes it's interesting to read through past journals to see how much I have improved, and how much my life has changed. It can also be humorous to look back on things that once seemed so serious, yet turned out to be trivial. One week I would be obsessing over cancer, the next it would be malaria. You often forget about these things unless you write them down.

So from today (or at the very most, tomorrow) make a promise to yourself that you will give yourself that 15 minutes. Write for two to three pages. And repeat each day.

Opening Up

It's a sad fact that mental health is a topic that still has so much stigma attached to it. It seems utterly ludicrous that someone could feel fine when telling their partner that they've broken their leg, yet feel unable to let them know that they have health anxiety, or depression, or bi-polar disorder. But the simple truth is, often explaining the problem takes a massive weight off of your shoulders, in that you no longer have to feel alone.

Sometimes it can be hard, I will admit that. I come from a family who never discuss mental health issues. Similarly, my friends never discuss things like that (being a bloke and discussing health in general is always a huge taboo!) But the truth is, even if you feel unable to approach your partner, your family or friends – there is always someone who will be able to listen, and comfort you.

Obviously my first recommendation would be to visit your GP, who may then recommend that you see a therapist who is trained in mental health issues. It's really nothing to worry about – as scary as it seems, therapists are there to help you. If you feel that your therapist does not understand what you are saying, you can always request to see someone else. As I have learnt from experience, it can take a couple of tries before you meet someone you can comfortably open up to.

The internet can be a double-edged sword. It can be like a goldmine for anxiety sufferers who want to 'symptom-surf'. At the same time, one other great source of support can come from internet forums.

In the early days of my recovery I found a great sense of satisfaction from posting on anxiety forums, as well as responding to other people in a similar situation. By helping others, you truly are helping yourself. One of the greatest health anxiety and panic forums I have found is at www.nomorepanic.co.uk. It is a lively, friendly and multi-cultural forum, and would happily give a personal recommendation for it's benefit. There are also several other boards around, which I will list in the resources section.

One word of warning, however: forums can potentially be triggering. They are often filled with people at the peak of their anxiety – and will often mention a multitude of symptoms and diseases. Its important to remember what you are taking part in forum discussions for; to help yourself and others with health anxiety – not to make things worse!

Daily Meditation

One of the lifestyle changes I made that I feel contributed greatly to my recovery was my habit of meditating on a daily basis. If you haven't tried it already, meditation is a great way to remove anxious tendencies and to clear your thoughts. It does take practice, though – don't expect to get it right the first time – but if you persist, you will no doubt start to see the benefits.

When you meditate, it is important that you are in a quiet place, with your mobile phone off, TV off and let yourself be free from distractions.

There are so many great meditation practices out there; simply way too many to list in this book. However, one good meditation I often practice is as follows:

Close your eyes and focus on your breathing. Without forcing yourself, try to breathe slowly and deeply. For each inhalation, think of something positive that you are bringing inside you. It can be anything at all; joy, confidence and love are things I commonly use. As you breathe in this positivity, see how it fills your entire body, starting in your lungs, but flowing around your body.

On the other side, when you exhale, think of all of the negative things that you are trying to get rid of. You might choose anxiety, anger, frustration, or any other negative force that you feel is controlling your life. When you breathe out, feel this negativity leave you. Imagine breathing out on a cold, frosty day – you can see your breath leave your body. I often use this image to help me visualise when meditating.

Meditation can be done at any time in the day, though I find it often works best as early as possible in the morning. I currently wake up at 5.30 to meditate for 20 minutes, then meditate again in the evening for another 20 minutes when I return from work. If possible, allocate a timeslot each day for your meditation. You won't regret it.

Exercise

It may seem like common sense, but a great way to alleviate stress and anxiety is regular exercise. I had heard it dozens of times and ignored the idea (mainly because I have always been lazy as sin!) but once I started exercising on a regular basis I found that it was helping me change not only emotionally, but physically.

Exercise makes you feel more confident, it gives you a sense of routine and as a sufferer of health anxiety, it feels good to know that you're doing something good for your health.

Sometimes it can be a challenge; sure, it's easier to stay in and watch TV. Often it's getting up and doing it that's the hardest part; in part, my local gym has a motto – on the outside door are the words '*you've just managed the hardest part.*' It's true. One you just get moving it's easy from there.

I would say the best forms of exercise to start off with are those that give you an all-body workout. Running is fantastic (though make sure you get a good pair of running shoes to avoid shin splints!) as well as swimming. If you haven't exercised for a long time you can start with a walk round the block. Make it a part of your routine and build up from there.

It's all about consistency. Get into an exercise routine, stick to it and you will surely start to see the benefits.

Diet

When I was at the height of my health anxiety, the food I was eating was absolutely awful. I would have takeaway pizza at least two times a week; the rest of the week would be a mix of fish and chips, omelettes, and if I was feeling super-healthy perhaps a home-cooked spaghetti bolognese, covered with cheese.

I was drinking alcohol every night – sometimes even as much as a bottle of wine. As you can imagine, this diet didn't have a particularly good effect on my health. I was overweight, unhappy and stressed. It was actually a move abroad that forced me to think about my diet. In 2008 I moved to Tokyo, Japan, to take an opportunity teaching. While living in Japan, I changed my diet so much that I came back weighing a stone less than when I arrived, feeling healthier than I ever had before. There are several aspects to the Japanese diet that are beneficial to a healthy lifestyle. Here are a few of them which I feel are worth sharing.

Green tea has been a prominent part of Japanese culture for hundreds of years. Japanese people drink plenty of the stuff, often after their meals. Green tea contains powerful anti-oxidants, and has long been considered as a way of helping improve one's mental health. It also has a number of other health benefits; many scientists and nutritionists have suggested green tea may assist in preventing cancer, diabetes, heart disease and skin ageing. I drink green tea on a daily basis – I actually prefer it to English tea! You can easily pick up green tea at supermarkets and health food stores over here – just try to find caffeine-free products where you can.

Cut down on dairy. While dairy products have become increasingly popular in Japan, particularly in the latter half of the 20th century, the Japanese dairy intake is still considerably lower than that of other countries, particularly the UK and USA. Dairy has been known to cause sinus issues, as well as heightened cholesterol. Instead of drinking milk, I often drink soya milk. It took a while to get used to the difference in taste, but I now love it and have it with everything – from a cup of tea to my morning cereal!

Eat smaller portions. One thing I noticed since coming back from Japan was the humungous size of meals in the UK. In Japanese culture, it's common to be presented with a variety of smaller dishes which you can help yourself to. That way, you can eat just the right amount for you without stuffing yourself silly – something we have a habit of doing in the Western world. Several studies have suggested that by eating smaller portions, you avoid bloating and give your digestive system a break – it can certainly help you lose a bit of weight as well!

Eat a lot of fish! I know that several of you are allergic to fish or simply do not like the taste. That's fine – there are certainly alternatives, but numerous studies have shown the correlation between eating fish and one's mental health. In particular, oily fish such as mackerel, sardines, fresh (not canned) tuna and even salmon have a high reputation for being excellent 'brain-boosters'.

I believe the logical piece of advice is to ensure that your diet is balanced and providing you with the nutrition to not only feed your body, but also your mind.

Avoiding caffeine

As an avid coffee enthusiast, cutting down on caffeine was an especially difficult task for me. After all, I loved waking up to the aroma of my morning coffee as it wafted through into the bedroom. However, I knew that if I was serious about conquering my anxiety, I had to cut down on my caffeine intake.

The problem is that drinking a lot of caffeinated drinks has been proven to exacerbate anxiety symptoms and can certainly affect the quality of your sleep.

When I first decided to give up coffee, I went cold turkey. I bought a load of decaffeinated tea and coffee and enthusiastically prepared myself for a caffeine-free life. The only trouble was, I found myself so grouchy and irritable at the end of my third day without coffee that I realised that simply cutting down may be a more sensible option!

Nowadays, I still enjoy my morning espresso but throughout the day I will balance this with decaffeinated coffee and green tea. I have also found that I have been drinking more water since cutting down on coffee, which I feel has given me more energy.

Taking Vitamins and Supplements

Taking multi-vitamins and supplements may also help, though it's always best to check with your GP as there are certain kinds that may interact with medication that you're taking. The vitamins I found best for anxiety are Vitamin B, Vitamin C and Vitamin D.

Vitamin B vitamins have long been seen as a great supplement to lower anxiety levels. Vitamins B6 (pyridoxine), B1 (thiamine) and B12 (cobalamin) have been seen as particularly effective. I personally take a B-Complex vitamin each night which I feel has given me extra energy.

You can also get Vitamin B from a number of food sources, from turkey and tuna, to lentils and beans.

It has been suggested that a **Vitamin C** deficiency can reduce our ability to handle stress and anxiety. As it's primarily found in fruit and veggies, it's important to make sure that your body is getting it's fair share of the stuff! We often associate oranges with having the highest vitamin C content but other great sources are strawberries, green peppers and kale.

Vitamin D comes from a number of food sources such as eggs and oily fish, but also from exposure to the sun's ultra-violet light. As anxiety sufferers may avoid leaving the comforts of their own home, it is no surprise that we may be deficient in this important vitamin. It is therefore important that we acquire this from other sources.

Your local health food store should be able to give you a wealth of guidance on vitamins and multi-vitamins.

As well as vitamins, many studies have shown the importance of supplements, ranging from fish oils to plant extracts. As with vitamins its always important to consult your GP or a pharmacist before taking any of these; St. John's

Wort in particular has been known to react with certain anti-depressants.

There are three supplements in particular that have been helpful for me over the years; Valerian Root, 5-HTP and fish oil.

Valerian Root

Valerian is a herbal remedy that is commonly taken as a way of aiding sleep, as well as relieving mild anxiety. It can be found in many of the herbal sleeping pills that you can find in high street chemists. Valerian can be taken in both tablet or liquid form, which you dilute with water. I must admit, the latter does smell quite foul but is less noticeable in a nice sugary cup of tea!

5-HTP

5-HTP (otherwise known as 5-Hydroxytryptophan – try to say that after a few pints!) is an amino acid which has commonly been used as a supplement for depression. However, many have seen some success in taking it for anxiety as well. After I stopped taking anti-depressants, I decided that I would try a number of natural remedies. 5-HTP certainly seemed to be one of the most successful in reducing my symptoms as well as improving the quality of my sleep.

Fish oil

Many studies have shown that fish oil supplements have the potential to reduce anxiety symptoms. While the taste of some of these supplements may be a put-off, they contain omega-3 fatty acids, which have long been seen as anxiety and depression busters. For those of you who do not eat fish, there are other great sources of omega-3 fatty acids on the market that you can find at good health food stores.

Part 4: Wrapping Things Up

"It is not in the stars to hold our destiny but in ourselves"
William Shakespeare

In this book I have presented a number of ideas and methods that have worked for me. Some of them may work wonders for you, while others may not be much help at all. Perhaps you are committed to meditating in the morning but still cannot find the time for your writing ritual. That's fine. The most important thing is that you are making your first steps to recovery, and no matter what those steps involve, it's something that you should feel proud of. So many people let anxiety dominate their lives yet let years go by before doing anything about it. The question you continually have to ask yourself is: why is it important that I try to kick the health anxiety habit now, instead of waiting a few days... a few months... or a few years?

There may well be times that you lapse; you may feel that you're making progress and then find yourself obsessively monitoring your pulse while watching TV, or perhaps another 'health anxiety' habit. My advice would be to not beat yourself up about it. We all slip up from time to time (at least, I know I do!) but the key is to tell yourself that you're not going to let it control you. Say it aloud if you like: *You're not going to win, you're not going to win, you're NOT going to win!* Don't be afraid to let your health anxiety know exactly where it stands.

I would encourage you to read some of the books and visit the websites I have listed in the Resources section at the end of the book. Many of these have provided me with a great deal of insight, and the inspiration to write this book.

And please don't hesitate to get in touch. Whether its a note about what stage you're at in your recovery or feedback about the book, you can always contact me by e-mail at info@healthanxietyhelp.com

Good luck!

Darren

Resources

Books

Overcoming Health Anxiety, David Veale and Rob Willson (2009)

Its Not All In Your Head: How Worrying About Your Health Could Be Making You Sick – And What You Can Do About It, Gordon J G Asmundson and Steven Taylor

Self-Help For Your Nerves, Claire Weekes

Tackling Health Anxiety: A CBT Handbook, Helen Tyrer

Websites

No More Panic - www.nomorepanic.co.uk

Anxiety UK - www.anxietyuk.org.uk

The Hypochondriac - http://www.thehypochondriac.com

Hypochondria Support Group -

http://www.dailystrength.org/c/Hypochondria/support-group

Other Books By Darren Sims

Conquering Procrastination: 50 Simple Steps To Get Off Your Butt and Get More Done
Available on Amazon stores.

Understanding Panic Attacks
Coming December 2014.

Made in the USA
Monee, IL
29 May 2020